Letterland

Contents

T0351718

Level 3 - Student Book 1

Review **Level 1** shapes and sounds with a 'Quick Dash' and complete the pages in *Workbook 1*, pages 2-23.

Track 2

Who is this?

What is her sound?

Review Level

1

Workbook

a b c d e f g h i j k l m

n o p q r s t u v w x y z

Review →

Review Level 2 content and consolidate learning by revisiting the language and songs <u>as necessary</u>.

Track 03

Sing

Workbook

Write

When Clever Cat is next to Harry, his hairy hat makes her sneeze, "ch!"

chin

chair

children

chicken

When Sammy Snake sits behind Harry, hissing 'sss', Harry turns back and says, "sh!"

fish

ship

shell

shoe

Track 04

Sing

Workbook

Write

Harry and Tess both think **that the** thunder is too loud. "Th!"

three

bath

path

throw

this	then	there
that	them	their
the	these	they

Track 05

Sing

Workbook

Write

Harry Hat Man laughs as he takes Peter Puppy's photo.

elephant

telephone

Track 06

Sing

Workbook

Write

photograph

dolphin

Walter whooshes Harry's hat off so Harry is too startled to speak.

wheel

wheat

Track 07

Sing

Workbook

Write

whale

whistle

Story time

The Fish Dish

1. Look at the pictures and see if you can guess what the story is about.
2. Read the story together.
3. Search for all the '**ch**', '**sh**', '**th**', '**ph**' and '**wh**' words.
4. See how much you can read!

Clever Cat was in the kitchen.

"What can I eat for lunch?" she said.

3

"I like fresh fish," Clever Cat said.

4

She put fish on her shopping list.

5

She went to the fish shop. It was shut.

6

She went to another shop. No fresh fish!

"Where can I get fresh fish?" she asked herself.

She went to three shops. No fresh fish!

Clever Cat went home to phone for help.

She did not see Fred.
Crash!

"Sorry, Fred. Is this your bag?" said Clever Cat.

"Yes. I went to catch three fish for you," said Fred.

"What? Fresh fish! Thank you so much!" she said.

"Now you can come for lunch!" said Clever Cat.

Magic e makes Mr A appear and say his name.

gate

cake

lake

grapes

Track 09
Sing
Workbook
Write

When Mr A and Mr I go out walking. Mr A does the talking.

rain

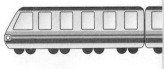
train

snail

paint

Track 10
Sing
Workbook
Write

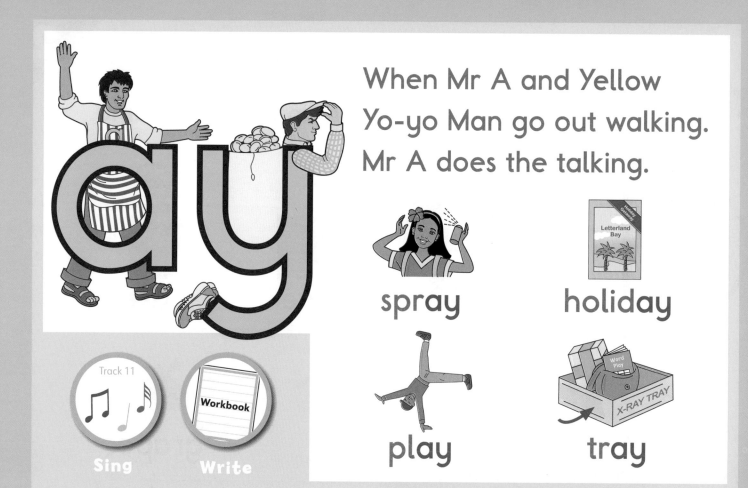

When Mr A and Yellow Yo-yo Man go out walking. Mr A does the talking.

spray

holiday

play

tray

Track 11

Workbook

Sing

Write

Review - Let's read!

Tim gets off the train. He plays in the rain.
Stay away from the train tracks!
Stay away from the wet paint on the gate!

Story time → **The Cave Escape**

1. Look at the pictures and see if you can guess what the story is about.
2. Read the story together.
3. Search for all the '**a_e**' words.
   Search for all the '**ai**' words.
   Search for all the '**ay**' words.
4. See how much you can read!

1

One day, Bouncy Ben, Clever Cat and Sammy Snake went on holiday.

2

They went to Letterland bay. They played games in the sand.

3

But then Bouncy Ben
lost his ball in a cave.

4

They went into the
cave to find the ball.

5

Ben was sad. "That ball
was a birthday present."

6

Then they saw waves
coming into the cave.

"Help! Help! We're afraid of the waves!"

"I can swim away and get help," said Sammy Snake.

"Let's stay at the back of the cave away from the spray."

Bouncy Ben and Clever Cat hate the waves.

"Hooray! Sammy Snake is coming to save us!"

"Thank you, Sammy. We won't play in caves again!"

As they escaped, Ben's ball came out of the waves! Ben had his ball again!

"We'll stay away from caves and waves on our next holiday!"

Magic e makes Mr E
appear and say his name.

delete

scene

athlete

compete

Track 13

Sing Write

When Mr E and his
brother go out walking.
Mr E does the talking.

tree

cheese

jeep

sleep

Track 14

Sing Write

When Mr E and Mr A go out walking, Mr E does the talking.

peach

meat

leaf

tea

Track 15

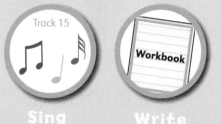

Workbook

Sing   **Write**

Yellow Yo-yo Man works for Mr E at the end of thousands of words.

family

party

teddy

puppy

Track 16

Workbook

Sing   **Write**

Story time ➤ **Greedy Seagulls!**  Track 17 **2**

1. Look at the pictures and see if you can guess what the story is about.
2. Read the story together.
3. Search for all the '**e_e**', '**ee**', '**ea**' and '**y** as e' words.
4. See how much you can read!

Mike had a letter from Sammy. "Please come and see me by the sea."

Mike arrived at three. "Let's go to the beach," said Sammy.

"Eek! The greedy seagulls scream and screech..."

"...They steal our picnic off the beach!" said Sammy.

"I'll stay on the beach and keep the seagulls away," said Mike.

So Sammy sailed on the sea and Mike stayed by a big, green tree.

When seagulls came
Mike snapped his teeth.

But Mike fell asleep in
the heat.

"Oh!" Mike screamed.
"Greedy seagulls have
eaten our treats!"

"I have a plan, Sammy,"
said Mike. "Just wait
and see!"

Mike put a feast at his feet and the seagulls came.

But Mike's meal was no treat, just bits of steel!

"Hooray! This feast is just for me! It's a meal I love to eat!"

"The seagulls can't compete, Sammy. They've gone, so let's eat!"

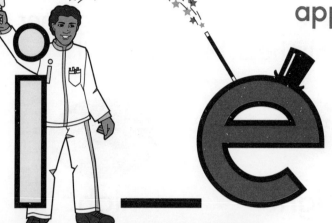

Magic **e** makes Mr I appear and say his name.

bike

slide

Track 18

♫ ♪
Sing

Workbook
Write

kite

lime

When Mr I and Mr E go out walking, Mr I usually does the talking.

pie

tie

flies

Track 19

♫ ♪
Sing

Workbook
Write

Rule breakers!

Mr I *usually* does the talking. But sometimes Mr E talks in words like:

field

When Mr I stands next to Golden Girl, he gives her an ice cream for being quiet. When these three are together you will only hear Mr I saying, 'I'.

light

night

fight

right

Track 20

Chant

Workbook

Write

At the end of some words we hear Mr I. But Mr I gets dizzy standing right at the end, so he asks Yo-yo Man to say 'i' for him, and thanks him with a big ice cream.

fly

sky

cry

why

Track 21

Chant

Workbook

Write

Story time  # High in the Sky!

1. Look at the pictures and see if you can guess what the story is about.
2. Read the story together.
3. Search for all the '**i_e**', '**ie**', '**igh**' and '**y** as i' words.
4. See how much you can read!

Kicking King went to fly his kite. The Queen stayed inside.

The wind was strong. He tried to fight it, but he let go of the kite.

The kite went high up into the sky.

"My kite! It's stuck in that pine tree!"

The King tried to get the kite, but it was quite high.

"I can jump as high as the sky," said Jumping Jim. "I can get the kite."

Jim jumped high but he did not get the kite.

"I will try to get the kite," said Noisy Nick.

Nick went up the pine tree, but it was so high.

Then Nick got stuck and began to cry.

The king went to get Firefighter Fred.

"My kite and Nick are stuck in a high pine tree."

Fred got Nick and the kite in no time. He smiled and said...

"...It's not a nice day to be flying kites so high!"

Magic e makes Mr O appear and say his name.

rose

phone

nose

rope

Track 23

Sing   Write   Workbook

When Mr O and Mr A go out walking, Mr O does the talking.

boat

goat

road

soap

Track 24

Sing   Write   Workbook

Mr O knows Walter Walrus plays splashing tricks, so he runs up to save Oscar shouting, "Oh no, you don't!"

Chant

Write

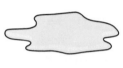
yellow

bowl

window

snow

Review - Let's read!

Can you see a boat?
Can you see a toad?
Can you see a toad hidden behind a rose?

Story time ➜ # The Bad Goat!

1. Look at the pictures and see if you can guess what the story is about.
2. Read the story together.
3. Search for all the '**o_e**' words.
   Search for all the '**oa**' words.
   Search for all the '**ow**' words.
4. See how much you can read!

Golden Girl likes to grow big green and yellow marrows.

But a goat got into the garden and ate the marrow! Bad goat!

"That marrow was for the Letterland show!"

"Go away from the garden. Bad, bad goat!"

The goat went slowly to the road. Kicking King went by in his coach.

The King stopped and spoke to Clever Cat. The goat ate his red coat!

Then the goat ate Clever Cat's yellow coat.

The goat went to the lake. Bouncy Ben sat in his boat.

The goat ate a rope. But Bouncy Ben needed the rope!

Then the goat went to an open window. Tess had made toast.

The goat ate the toast. Bad, bad goat!

The goat then went to the Letterland show.

"This goat wins the cup for the best goat," said a man in a yellow coat.

"That's my goat!" said Golden Girl. The goat then ate the man's coat!

u or oo

Magic e makes Mr U appear and say his name.

flute

cube

perfume

tube

Track 27

Sing

Workbook

Write

u or oo

When Mr U and Mr E go out walking, Mr U does the talking.

blue

glue

argue

Fondue Party!
Venue:
Bluebell Avenue
Tuesday

Tuesday

Track 28

Sing

Workbook

Write

The Boot and Foot Twins always fight. The Boot Twin says, "Oo, I've got your boots!"

balloon

zoo

spoon

boot

Track 29

Sing

Workbook

Write

Eddy knows Walter's tricks so he squirts water first! Walter cries, "ew!"*

news

jewels

chew

stew

Track 30

Sing

Workbook

Write

*The sound you hear can either be an 'oo' (as in chew) or 'you' (as in new).

Story time ➤ New Blue Jeans

1. Look at the pictures and see if you can guess what the story is about.
2. Read the story together.
3. Search for all the 'u_e', 'ue', 'oo' and 'ew' words.
4. See how much you can read!

* Teach the word 'they' as it is a high usage word. They will meet the Letterland character to explain the sound later in Level 3.

On Tuesday afternoon Max went to see Nick.

Nick had on his new, blue jeans.

*They drew big rockets, zooming into space.

"Let's make a rocket with these tubes and glue," said Nick.

Nick put the glue on a stool. "I must not get glue on my new jeans!" he said.

They glued lots of tubes and made a huge rocket.

"Let's add these tubes, too!" said Nick.

They painted it blue. "Don't get it on your new jeans!"

"It looks just like the rocket we drew!" said Max.

Then Nick slipped on the tube of blue paint...

Max ran to help but fell on the stool!

The pot of glue flew off the stool!

"It's OK," said Nick. "No paint or glue got on my new, blue jeans."

"That's true!" said Max. "But just look at the room!"

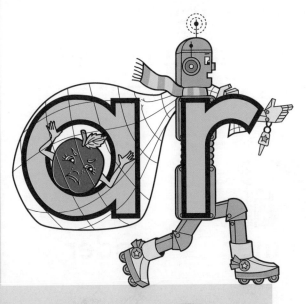

Arthur Ar steals apples.
As he runs off he
shouts, "Ar!"

Sing   Write

Track 32   Workbook

car

stars

scarf

card

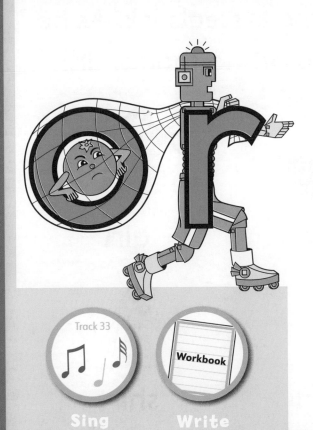

Orvil Or steals oranges.
As he runs off he
shouts, "Or!"

Track 33   Workbook

Sing   Write

fork

horse

sport

storm

Ernest Er steals elephants. As he runs off he shouts, "Er!"

hammer

ladder

tiger

painter

Track 34

Sing

Workbook

Write

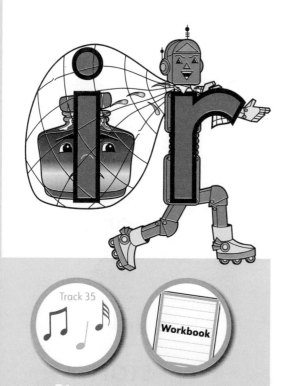

Irving Ir steals ink. As he runs off he shouts, "Ir!"

bird

girl

skirt

shirt

Track 35

Sing

Workbook

Write

Urgent Ur steals umbrellas. As he runs off he shouts, "Ur!"

nurse

purse

burger

purple

Track 36

Sing   Write

Red Robot captures Walter in his sack. Walter is too startled to speak.

write

wreck

wring

wrapper

Track 37

Sing   Write

Curled in Fur

1. Look at the pictures and see if you can guess what the story is about.
2. Read the story together.
3. Search for all the '**ar**', '**er**', '**ir**', and '**ur**' words.
4. See how much you can read!

Two little kittens are drinking milk for their dinner. The black kitten is Arthur. His sister is Martha.

After their milk they curl up together.

They like to sleep in the fur of their mother.

But then, mother asks, "Are you fast runners?"

Martha and Arthur race to be first.

6

Then Arthur and
Martha play like tigers!

7

Is Arthur or Martha the
better fighter?

8

Then they curl up
in a circle to sleep.

9

But when they wake
up they can't see their
mother.

A girl picks them up.
She is their owner.

"Let's put you back with
your mother, little tigers."

Arthur and Martha are pleased to be back with their
mother. Curled up in her fur, they start to purr.

Oscar's Bothersome Little Brother can't say, 'o' like Oscar. Instead he just says, 'uh'.

monkey

money

dove

honey

Track 39

Workbook

Chant　Write

The Foot Twin says, "Oo, just look at my foot!"

wood

book

wool

foot

Track 40

Workbook

Sing　Write

Umbrellas that are pushed and pulled into letters don't make their usual sound.

push

pull

sugar

cushion

Review - Let's read!

I love honey.

If you have money.

You can get honey and make a lovely honey cake from the cookbook.

Roy and Yo-yo Man play the 'Oy game' at the end of words.

toys

boy

annoyed

soy

Track 42

Workbook

Write

Roy and Mr I play the 'Oi game' inside words.

boil

oil

soil

coins

Track 43

Workbook

Sing   Write

Story time → **Lots to Enjoy!**

1. Look at the pictures and see if you can guess what the story is about.
2. Read the story together.
3. Search for all the **o**, **oo**, **u**, **oi** and **oy** words.
4. See how much you can read!

It was cold and wet outside, and the Queen was annoyed.

"I can't enjoy my garden," she said, "so I'm going out to spend money."

3

The King joined Clever Cat in her cottage and explained the problem.

4

Clever Cat sat on her cushion, thinking of ways to help.

5

She put on her wool scarf and her boots.

6

Then, she went on foot to look at the Queen's garden.

"I think I have a clever idea to help the Queen enjoy her garden."

"The Queen loves her swing. Let's brush the leaves and pull up the weeds!"

The King then painted the wood and put oil on the swing.

"Let's cover it up so it will be a surprise!" said Clever Cat.

When the Queen came home, the King made her cover her eyes and took her to the garden.

"Look! We want you to enjoy spring in your garden!" said the King.

The Queen pointed her finger at them, but this time she was not annoyed.

"I love it, and I love you!" she said.

When Walter splashes Annie Apple she cries "Aw! Don't be so awful!".

jigsaw

yawn

paw

saw

Walter hides in Uppy's letter and splashes Annie Apple. She cries "Au! Don't be so awful!".

autumn

astronaut

saucer

launch

Track 45

Chant

Write

Workbook

Track 46

Chant

Write

Workbook

1. Look at the pictures and see if you can guess what the story is about.
2. Read the story together.
3. Search for all the **aw** words.
   Search for all the **au** words.
4. See how much you can read!

Granny had a pink and black shawl and a handbag that matches.

Then for her birthday we gave her a little dog. His name was Paul.

3

Granny hugged Paul and stroked his paws!

4

She filled his kennel on the lawn with soft, fresh straw.

5

She played games with Paul on the lawn.

6

But then Granny went and left her shawl on the lawn.

Paul saw the shawl.
He saw it as a toy!

He grabbed the shawl
between his paws.

Then he played with it
on the lawn. Paul had
fun with the shawl!

But then Granny saw
him. "No! Naughty Paul!
Just look at my shawl!"

"Your paws and claws have ripped my shawl!"

"How awful! Naughty, Paul," she said.

Granny was sad. Now she had no shawl to match her pink and black bag.

"It's OK. I have another shawl, but there's no other dog like Paul!"

Walter bumps his chin as he splashes Oscar. They both howl, "Ow!"

vowels

cow

town

shower

Track 48
Sing   Write

Walter bumps his chin as he splashes Oscar. They both howl, "Ou!".

mouse

fountain

mountain

house

Track 49
Sing   Write

Story time ➤ **The Loud Crowd**

1. Look at the pictures and see if you can guess what the story is about.
2. Read the story together.
3. Search for all the **ow** words. Search for all the **ou** words.
4. See how much you can read!

"I need a new song," said the King. "And it must be a loud song," he shouted!

The music man went to his house and tried to think of some loud sounds.

He sang his song to the King. "It must be louder!"

The man looked around for a new, loud sound.

Back in town the King sat on his bed. He held his crown and frowned.

He could think of lots of quiet sounds but no very loud sounds!

The music man looked up, down and around.

He got his coat and went out into town.

In the town there was a crowd. They were playing quiet music.

But when they all played together the sound was loud. That gave the man an idea!

He spoke to the crowd. They went to the King's house.

The crowd came in and played for the King...

The crowd made lots more sounds. Together they were very, very loud!

"Thank you!" shouted the King. "It's my loud, town crowd!"

Story ➔ Let's see what happens when a robot captures these two Vowel Men.

Track
51

Robot tricks!

When Mr A and Mr I go out walking, Mr A does the talking.
Mr I looks out for robots who might want to capture them.

But sometimes, Mr I does not spot the robot in time! The robot captures both Vowel Men in his sack. They are heavy, so the robot puffs out air and says, "I've caught a pair! I need air!"

Letter sounds Use your *Picture Code Cards* to review Mr A, Mr I and Arthur Ar's sounds. Then look at the new sound they make when they are together.

63

Explore → Listen to the story about this robot capturing Vowel Men.

Track 52

Mr A, Mr I and a Robot

3 letters: 1 sound

Listen again and this time look for the things in the picture that have the 'air' sound.

Find these items in the picture. Listen for the 'air' sound in the middle and at the end of the words.

Track 53

fair

hair

chair

stairs

fairy

Workbook

When you have finished this page, do the Keywords exercises on pages 54-55, *Workbook 1*.

Workbook

a pair = 2

a pair of boots

a pair of socks

a pair of gloves

Listen to the song!

Ha, ha, ha! I've caught a pair
of Vowel Men walking by.
It's tough to carry both of them,
so you will hear me sigh.

I need lots of air!
Because I've caught a pair!

Oh, this is not fair!
Find me a chair!" (x2)

Song

Listen to the song. If you can, join in when you listen for the
second time.

Word Building Build some **air** words using the *Software, Letter Sound Cards*, or the *Picture Code Cards*.

Code Card

Build it!

air, hair, fair, pair
stairs, chair.

Let's read! Use the Sound Slide trick to blend the sounds together and read the words. Then try reading the sentences with more fluency.

The fairy is on
the chair.

I use a hairbrush
on my hair.

Pair work

Work in pairs. Read the sentences to a partner as fluently as
you can. Then complete pages 56-57, *Workbook 1*.

Workbook

67

Track 56

Robot tricks!

When Mr E and Mr A go out walking, Mr E does the talking.
Mr A looks out for robots who might want to capture them.

Sometimes, Mr A does not spot a robot in time!
The robot captures both Vowel Men in his sack.

There are two sounds you might hear when you see these two Vowel Men behind a robot's back.

(1) The robot puffs out hot **air** because they are

(2) heavy.

The Vowel Men make lots of noise when they are caught. The robot pretends not to hear. He points to his **ear** and says, "can't h**ear**!"

Letter sounds Use your *Picture Code Cards* to review Mr E, Mr A and Ernest Er's sounds. Then look at the new sound they make when they are together.

**Explore**

Listen to the story about how this robot captures vowels. He makes two sounds: one sounds like 'ear' the other sounds like 'air'.

Track 57

Mr E, Mr A and a Robot

**3 letters: 1 sound**

Listen again and this time look for the things in the picture that have the '**ear**' sound.

Find these items in the picture. Listen for the 'ear' sound at the end of the words.

hear

spear

ear

pear

bear

tear

Workbook — When you have finished this page, do the Keywords exercises on pages 58-59, *Workbook 1*.

Workbook

Listen to the song. If you can, join in when you listen for the second time.

Track 59

Listen to the song!

Oh dear! Oh dear!
That cheeky robot's too near!
He's caught Mr E and Mr A.
And the robot is pretending not to hear!

"I can't hear you! I can't hear you.
Even when you shout into my ear!"

But the weight is too much for the robot to bear,
and he starts to think about the wear and tear.

"I can't bear it! I can't bear it!
I need to puff out some air."

Ear! Air! Ear! Air!

Search and read Do not try to read the whole song, but can you read the words that have the Robot stealing Vowel Men in them?

71

Build some **ear** words using the *Software, Letter Sound Cards,* or the *Picture Code Cards.*

Code Card

Build it!

ear, beard,
clear, hear,
near, spear, year.

bear, pear
tear, wear.

Let's read!

Use the Sound Slide trick to blend the sounds together and read the words. Then try reading the sentences with more fluency.

There is a tear in the T-shirt I am wearing.

I think these bears like pears.

Pair work Work in pairs. Read the sentences to a partner as fluently as you can. Then complete pages 60-61, *Workbook 1.*

I went to the today.

I went on a slide, then watched

Mr E. He was doing a magic

trick. At 1 o'clock I was hungry.

I saw a and sat down.

I got out a picnic to eat. Then I

could a very loud sound.

Slurp! Slurp! Slurp!

What is that sound? I looked at

the next to me. There was

a eating his lunch, too!

He was eating a very ripe !

pear

chair

bear

fair

hear

Let's read This activity allows you to make the connection between the image and the written word. Now listen to the story.

Track 60

73

Story time

A Day Trip to the Zoo

1. Look at the pictures and discuss what the story might be about.
2. Read the story together.
3. Search for all the 'air' and 'ear' words.
4. See how much you can read!

Annie Apple is visiting the animals at the zoo. Is there a zoo near you?

She visits the alligator to hear it's snapping teeth.

She visits an anteater. He licks an ant off near her ear!

Reading

Fluency - Reading fluently is a skill which can be achieved through familiarity with the text. Listen, then read the story.

Track 61

Bouncy Ben is at the zoo, too. He goes to the zoo once a year. He's so happy he jumps high in the air!

He visits a buffalo and a big brown bear. He can see them so clearly.

Clever Cat is visiting the camels. Talking Tess is talking to a tiger. She likes the tiger's stripes. She thinks the stripes look like her hair.

Now try writing

When you have finished this page, do the related **Day Trip to the Fair** exercise on pages 62-63 of *Workbook 1*.

Workbook

Stickers  Complete the sticker activity in *Workbook 1*, page 64.

Listen Complete the exercise in *Workbook 1*, page 65.

Talk time Listen to the conversation.
Then you try asking a partner about their holidays.

Track 63

Land, Sea or Air?

Questions	Answers
Have you been on holiday this year?	Yes, I have. No, I haven't.
Where did you go? Where did you go last year?	I went to... (places/location)
What did you see?	I saw...
What did you do?	I went (to the beach/cycling/climbing/to a museum/to the city)
How did you travel?	I went by land/sea/air. I travelled by (boat/train/car/airplane)

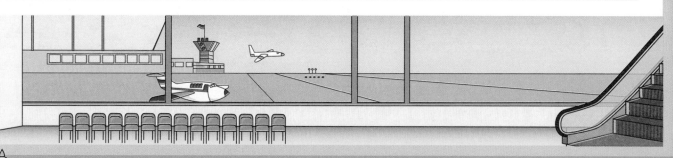

Pair work Work in pairs. Ask each other about their travels. Then tell the rest of the class what you have been talking about!

Story ➜

Clever Cat likes to make a different sound in some words. Listen.

Track 64

Blue magic!

Clever Cat's secret is she loves to hiss like Sammy Snake, so Mr E invented Blue Magic!

When Clever Cat sits next to an e, an i or a y, Blue Magic sparks appear! The sparks are just strong enough to turn Clever Cat into a hissing snake for a little while... sssssss.

Letter sounds Use your *Picture Code Cards* to review Clever Cat's usual sound. Then look at the new sound she likes to make when she is next to certain letters.

77

 **Explore**

Listen to the story about what happens when Clever Cat comes into contact with Blue Magic sparks.

Track 65

Clever Cat as a hissing snake

Letter sounds

Listen again and this time look for the things in the picture that have the '**ce**', '**ci**' or '**cy**' sound.

Keywords

Find these items in the picture. Listen out for Clever Cat making a hissing sound in these words.

Track 66

face

space

city

circle

bicycle

cylinder

Workbook

There are specific *Workbook 1* pages for **ce**, **ci**, and **cy**. Spend up to three lessons completing pages 66-73.

Workbook

79

Listen to the song!

Watch out! Take care!

Blue Magic's in the air!

It comes flying out of vowels all the time.

It's nice to see, and

between you and me,

it gives Clever Cat a chance to really shine.

The Blue Magic sparks land right on her face!

So she turns from a cat to a snake!

She hisses so loud, you'll hear her in space,

and she's sure to keep the city wide awake!

Ssss....

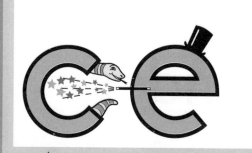
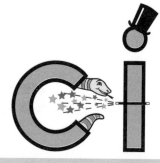

Search and read Do not try to read the whole song, but can you read the words that have the Blue Magic in them?

Build some **ce** words using the *Picture Code Cards, Letter Sound Cards* or *Software.*

Code Card

Build it!

ice, nice, mice, rice
ace, face, lace.

Let's read! ➤

Use the Sound Slide trick to blend the sounds together and read the words. Then try reading the sentences with more fluency.

Call an ambulance.
It's an emergency!

The mice like to dance
on the fence.

He needs ice on his face.

Pair work

Work in pairs. Read the sentences to a partner as fluently as you can.

Story time

Grocery Shopping!

1. Look at the pictures and discuss what the story might be about.
2. Read the story together.
3. Search for all the '**ce**', '**ci**' and '**cy**' words.
4. See how much you can read!

Sammy Snake is grocery shopping in the city for his supper. "I want something really nice," he says.

"I like soup. I like juicy satsumas, too." he says.

"Oh look at this nice, fresh fish on ice."

 Reading

Comprehension - Talk about the story and ask questions. Children can be too busy decoding words to understand what they are reading.

 Track 68

"I like spicy samosas and salad, too. But is salad really nice?" he says.

It's so hard to choose when the grocery store is full of excellent food.

"Spaghetti! I can add spice and I can eat it with salmon and salad! Lucy! I have lots of space at my place. Come and have nice, spicy spaghetti with me tonight!" he says.

Now try writing

When you have finished this page, do the related **Grocery Shopping** exercises on pages 74-75 of *Workbook 2*.

Stickers ➤ Complete the sticker activity in *Workbook 1*, page 76.

Listen ➤ Complete the exercises in *Workbook 1*, page 78-79.

Talk time ➤ Listen to this conversation.
Then you try asking a partner about space.

Track 71

Space

Questions	Answers
If you could go into space, would you go?	Yes, I would go. (It would be interesting/exciting.) No, I wouldn't go. (It would be scary/dangerous.)
If you could go into space, where would you go?	I would go to the moon. I would go to a planet. (Mercury, Venus, Mars, Jupiter, Saturn, Uranus, Neptune)
What do you think it would be like in space?	I think it would be hot/cold/windy/quiet in space. I think it would be dry and dusty in space.

Pair work Work in pairs. Ask each other about space. Use a dictionary to look up new words to descibe space.